NATURE CURE FOR PROSTATE TROUBLES

This book explains clearly why prostate troubles are so prevalent among middle-aged men, and how they may be overcome by a course of simple self-treatment without resorting to difficult and hazardous surgery.

Nature Cure for Prostate Troubles

Harry Clements N.D., D.O.

THORSONS PUBLISHERS LIMITED
Wellingborough, Northamptonshire

First published 1954
Ninth Impression 1972
Second Edition, revised and reset,
January 1974
Second Impression December 1974
Third Impression 1975
Fourth Impression 1977
Fifth Impression 1978
Sixth Impression 1981

ISBN 0 7225 0246 X (paperback)
ISBN 0 7225 0359 8 (hardback)

Photoset by Specialised Offset Services Ltd., Liverpool
Printed and bound in Great Britain by
Richard Clay (The Chaucer Press) Ltd.,
Bungay, Suffolk.

Contents

Introduction

It is true to say that every middle-aged man looks forward, with real apprehension, towards prostate trouble in his old age. It has become so much of a commonplace complaint that, just as many parents think that tonsil-cutting is a requisite to a normal life, aging men have a similar outlook on the operation for the removal of the prostate gland. This point of view is advocated by the medical profession in general. Sometime ago an American magazine, which is sponsored by the American Medical Association, carried an article that stated this point of view quite frankly, and any middle-aged man who might have read that article would have accepted the idea that his chances of escaping this major operation were very slight indeed. There was not the faintest hint in the article that preventive measures might be of any value, and the only consolation for the inevitability of the operation that was offered was the fact that men lived longer and thus the operation became one of the penalties of the increased span of life.

The acceptance of this attitude carries with it quite naturally the hope that surgical operations, if they become absolutely necessary, may be carried out with a maximum degree of safety, and there is little doubt that this condition has been achieved. The advance made in anaesthetics and the improved aseptic technique has made the work of the surgeon so safe, in the short-term sense, that no one need fear the outcome. They have given the surgeon time to perform what he has to do, and considering the thousands of operations that are now performed there is only the occasional accident to be accounted for. Those who have achieved this result point with pride to it and glory in the surgical progress of modern times.

The safety of surgery is a popular theme in the daily press, and thus people are being constantly conditioned to feel that if it becomes necessary at least the dangers and the horrors of old-time surgery have been eliminated. In recent years, surgery has developed to the point where transplantation of heart, lungs and other vital organs are commonplace events in the life of the ordinary individual. In view of these achievements the removal of the prostate becomes mere surgical child's play in the hands of the up-to-date surgeon.

MILLIONS OF OPERATIONS

Millions will undergo operations within the next year and quite a few will be for the removal of the prostate gland in aged and ageing men, and unless something is done of a constructive nature outside the field of surgery the number will increase with each passing year. There is, of course, all that goes with hospitalization, the staff and the general upkeep, and probably the average operation means at least from a week to three weeks in such institutions. Add to this the loss of time involved, and then on the top of this the number of surgeons and auxiliaries, and we get some idea of what society faces as a necessary corollary of modern living.

Leaving aside the actual money transactions in such affairs – and the amount involved must be colossal – the whole thing must involve a great economic strain in which a proportion of the people will be fully engaged in taking surgical care of the rest of the community. On the figures we have just

quoted the strain is big enough, but when we realize
that with each succeeding year the figures are sub-
stantially increased we get some idea of the difficulties the future holds for a society that thinks, not
in terms of prevention, but in terms of surgical treatment.

STORY OF TONSILS

It is of interest to speculate on what may happen if
surgical progress continues at its present rate. Given a
free hand, there is hardly any limit to its scope. No
family can hope to grow up without availing itself of
its benefits, from the tonsils in early life to the prostate in old age. Fortunately these things seem to have
a knack of adjusting themselves, and if we take some
pointers from history we may draw some conclusion
as to what may happen in the future. The story of the
tonsils is a good starting point. For many years now
the surgeons have worked on them with a will, and, as
everybody knows, their removal has been held to be a
grim necessity to prevent all kinds of diseases, from
colds and fevers to rheumatism. By the time the
physicians and surgeons had satisfied themselves that
they were hunting a lost cause, the patients themselves, or, as in this case, the parents, were more convinced than the surgeons; so that when the latter
began to have their doubts the pressure came from
the laymen.

We observe this curious position at the present
time. The doctors are putting the tonsil cases on a
waiting list, hoping that in time the need for operation will be forgotten, or that, as is usually the case,
in the matter of a few months the condition will have
righted itself. But the parents find it less easy to
change their minds, and they are going from hospital
to hospital surreptitiously adding their children's
names to the waiting lists so that no chance will be

lost. The only satisfactory solution would be for the
medical profession to proclaim that the wholesale
removal of tonsils has been a shocking mistake, and
that they had been the victims of a false belief that
they caused all kinds of diseases and interfered with
the normal development of the rest of the body.

SURGERY NOT ESSENTIAL

We believe that the same thing may happen with the
prostate gland, and that there is an urgent necessity at
the present time to call attention to the fact that the
surgical removal of it is not the only solution. We do
not say that there are not cases where, after years of
wrong management and neglect, such treatment may
be necessary and justifiable; but they are and should
remain the exceptions. What we know for certain is
that many people are able to live to old age and not
be bothered in any way by prostatic troubles. From
this we may argue that it is self-evident that nature
has made the provision for its normal functioning
throughout life, and it is due to human errors that a
breakdown occurs.

From this premise we see the possibility of maintaining normal function so that surgical interference
will not become an inevitable consequence of growing
old. As with all the other organs in the body, what we
must concern ourselves with is the health of the body
as a whole. Because we have focused attention on
the various parts of the body and their afflictions we
mislead ourselves when we make any attempt to
institute preventive or curative measures. This same
attitude has given rise to the surgical assaults that
have been made on the tonsils, the prostate and other
organs. But attacking organs in this way merely
makes it impossible that normal function will ever
again be restored.

It is always more spectacular to do things than to

make them unnecessary, and that is why those who perform operations receive so much applause and approbation from the public. Some day, we think, the public will see that this is the completely wrong attitude to take so far as disease is concerned. It is all very well to merit attention by cutting out organs, by transplanting them and performing other marvellous feats with them, but it is far wiser to take care of them so that the normal course of life may be run with all of them intact.

I.
Structure and Function

The ordinary reader is interested in his body and its organs only inasmuch as such information may enable him to act intelligently in the normal course of life. Our description of the prostate gland and its functions will be limited to that degree, and no unnecessary detail will be entered into. What we describe will, however, be essential knowledge that will help the reader to understand why certain treatments have to be applied when the normal function of the gland has been upset.

DESCRIPTION OF PROSTATE GLAND

The prostate gland is a male organ, and anatomists in describing it have likened it to a large chestnut, which it resembles in shape and in colour, being reddish brown in appearance. It measures approximately one inch and a half in width and about an inch or so in length. It is separated laterally, as it were, so that two not very distinct lobes are formed. It is situated at the base of the bladder and around the commencement of the urethra, the membranous tube for the passage of the urine. The important point to observe at this stage is that it is vital in relation to the emptying of the bladder and bears a close relationship to the rectum. Later, when discussing disturbances of function and effective treatment, these points will be brought into clearer relief.

It is composed of both glandular and muscular tissue, and here, again, we should make special note of this fact, because the general impression is abroad that it is, as we say, a prostate gland. We make this point because all organs share in the general welfare of the body, and one that is both muscular and glandular will take on the conditions that are represented in both these bodily systems. When an enlargement takes place, as is so often the condition in which prostatic complaints are founded, the neglected muscles as much as the toxic glandular condition should be taken into consideration.

NUTRITION AND DRAINAGE

All muscular and glandular tissues in the body are supplied with nerves and blood vessels, and this applies to the prostate gland. The reason for this is not only that the parts may be activated and supplied with nutriment, but also that the waste products of cell activity should be disposed of. In all glandular tissue, in particular, it is important that this function is constantly maintained, and any retention of these products beyond the normal period is bound to be fraught with disturbance of function. The prostate gland is therefore richly supplied with arteries for carrying the nutritive elements, and also with lymph and veins for drainage purposes.

The veins are of especial importance in disorders of the prostate gland because they tend to varicosity.

Many people, as they grow old, develop varicosity of the veins on the lower parts of the body and legs, and this is due to the fact that the valves of the veins have become incompetent. The flow of the blood through the veins depends to a great extent, in some parts of the body, on the efficiency of the valves of the veins, and when they go out of action the veins enlarge and the blood flow is impeded.

Sufficient has been said about the structure and nature of the prostate gland to show that it is its relationship to the bladder and the passage of the urine that makes any change in its structure of such great importance. If, as is generally the case, the enlargement presses on the urethra and impedes the flow of the urine, then there is trouble ahead. The crux of the matter then is in relation to the change in structure and not so much in relation to the actual function of the gland itself.

2.

Causes of Prostate Disorders

The prevailing idea that surgical interference is the only way to meet the problems of the enlarged and obstructing prostate gland clearly rules out, for most people, the need to look for causes. But if the reader has read the foregoing chapter dealing with the structure and relative position of the gland he will be able to realize that very much may be done along those lines, and that the old adage, 'an ounce of prevention is worth a ton of cure,' is particularly applicable to this case.

As we have already seen, the trouble is largely a question of hypertrophy, which means that there has been an overgrowth of the normal tissue. Such an overgrowth might mean very little in another part of the system, but at this junction it can clearly interfere with an important function. Now overgrowth of such a nature is generally preceded by congestion. Such congestion may be a long drawn-out affair and give few warning signals until the result of it may be felt, as in the case of the prostate gland. But in congestion certain events accompany it. First of all there is an increased blood supply, and the tissue becomes unbalanced so far as nutrition and elimination are concerned. We think it is at this point that the trouble really begins.

TISSUE LIFE

Let us think for a few minutes of the necessary requirements of normal tissue life, because in so doing we can get an idea of what happens when things go wrong. All the tissues of the body need a proper supply of blood to carry the food elements, and the body also needs channels through which the waste products of its own activity must be carried away. Suppose that this equilibrium is upset. Suppose that the blood is sluggish and toxic and overloaded with enforced nutrition from a digestive system which is also overloaded and keeping up a pressure on the blood stream. Suppose that in addition to this the lymph and the veins that carry away the waste products are also overloaded and sluggish. The result will be that the tissues of the particular organ involved will be forced to retain the waste products of their own activity for a prolonged period. The further result will be that the tissues must retain and store them in the tissues. Now all toxic products of such a nature are stimulating and they tend to accelerate the functions of the various cells. The response is likely to be an overgrowth of normal tissue. Once this process has started there is no knowing where it will end, especially if the patient belongs to that school of thought that believes that he can correct such compensating actions of the system by taking a bottle of medicine.

In the prostate, as we have seen, there is a rich supply of glandular tissues, surrounded and permeated by muscular fibres. Glandular tissue is particularly liable to overgrowth following congestion. We can see with our eyes, in the case of the enlarged tonsils in the throat, where the same factors may be at work in early life as they will be later in the case of prostate enlargement. In the case of the prostate gland the enlargement of the glandular tissue will have its effects upon the muscular tissues, and these will be stretched and strained.

WASTE PRODUCTS

The factors we have described in relation to the intake and outgoing of food and waste products affect the whole of the body, so that the muscles of the prostate gland retain within themselves the waste products that lead to a lack of tone and the formation of heavily laden connective tissue. These muscles no longer carry out their normal function of contraction and relaxation and a pump-like action to keep the enclosed glandular tissue healthy.

The blood vessels and the lymph channels also become involved. The veins in particular will undergo changes as a result of the inefficiency of the muscular fibres and the congestion of the glandular tissues. Varicosity of the veins will develop, and this condition has often been seen in the gland when it has been removed by operation. This condition is not unlike the condition we are able to see in the legs, and is closely related to the condition that we describe as haemorrhoids or piles. As a matter of fact one can be practically certain that the sufferer from prostate trouble will suffer from haemorrhoids, and their presence should be a warning signal to men who are middle-aged or older. As we shall see later, a good deal of effective treatment that will be applied will affect the circulation in the legs and the rectum, and be just as effective in relieving the one condition as the other.

DIETETIC IMPLICATIONS

The foregoing remarks lead us directly to the conclusion that prostatic troubles are closely related to the digestive tract and that feeding and dieting are important matters that will have to be thought about when we are considering causative factors. Behind the congestive conditions that we have described we have the processes of digestion and assimilation, and what we eat and drink will have a direct bearing on the whole subject. The habit of eating three or four meals a day, and keeping them up through middle life as though the body still required the same amount of food as when it was in the formative stage, has led to many of our troubles.

We should remember that each meal adds to the pressure within the blood stream, and that the system must dispose of excess nutriment somewhere. When we are young and in full possession of our muscular vigour we may work off some of this excess food, but as we grow older, and we are less inclined to use our bodies, we are merely wasting the food and using up our energy in disposing of it. The plain fact is that habit has become the dominating factor in our lives, and by the time we reach middle age or older we act under their influence without any conscious thought. How often does the middle-aged man ask himself whether his body requires the twenty-one or more meals that he imposes on it in the course of a week?

Such overfeeding is one of the important causes that we must consider in such troubles as the one under discussion. It is not done wantonly; it is done thoughtlessly, but there is no doubt that restraint is perhaps the most important act of self-discipline that we must impose on ourselves if the system is showing signs of nutritional strain, and we insist that prostatic trouble is a definite sign of such a strain.

BOWEL ACTION

We rank, then, the feeding habits as being a primary contributing cause in every case of this nature, and later we shall indicate just how these errors should be rectified. But there is also another cause for the trouble, which, although related to the digestive tract, is of a mechanical nature. The position of the prostate gland makes it susceptible to pressure from sluggishness of the bowel action, and this may well act as an irritating cause of a great deal of congestion. Earlier we pointed out the relationship of the gland to the rectum, and when the faeces are slow in passing from this part of the bowel they may cause direct pressure on the gland and the surrounding blood vessels and other tissues.

This pressure is so direct that there are many patients who notice that the glandular secretion may be passed with the urine, and this should be regarded as a danger signal that needs careful watching. An occasional bout of constipation may do no permanent harm, but when it persists over months and years the local effect on the gland is bound to make itself felt. And almost as great an irritant may be the laxative medicines that are so often used for the correction of this condition. These medicines often cause irritation and congestion in the tissues of the rectum, and they spread in time to the prostate gland. Bad feeding habits, the sluggishness of the bowels that usually accompanies them, plus the use of laxative drugs is a chain of events that may account for prostate troubles and a lot more beside.

SEDENTARY OCCUPATION

Another factor that plays a part in making this chain of events more effectively operative is a sedentary occupation. Perhaps one should widen this definition these days, because a sitting occupation is not the only one that carries with it the dangers of immobilizing the abdominal and pelvic regions of the body — the condition that predisposes to prostatic troubles. There are many standing occupations that place a very great strain upon these parts of the body, and, indeed, one may say that constant standing may be of greater difficulty in this respect than any other position of the body.

Sitting and standing in set positions for long periods of time has a direct effect upon the circulation of the body and particularly upon the venous system. This fact is well recognized in the condition known as varicose veins, and also in haemorrhoidal complaints, but it is not so clearly understood in prostatic troubles. Yet, as we have shown, the veins of that structure are liable to varicosity, and the same factors that cause the trouble in the legs and the rectum will tend to produce it in the prostate gland.

The position of the prostate gland makes it particularly vulnerable in this way. Situated, as it is, in the lower abdomen, it must be affected by the constant downward pressure of the abdominal organs, and even in the best of circumstances this pressure may be very real. We should remember that the diaphragm, which separates the contents of the abdomen from those of the chest, is constantly pressing down on these organs, and when we cough or sneeze this pressure may become explosive and exert a great amount low down in the pelvis where the gland is situated. The young man, who is athletic and lissom, and without undue fat about his muscles, will clearly not suffer from this natural activity, but it is a very different matter for the middle-aged man who has, perhaps, spent a good deal of his working life sitting and standing in one strained position.

SAGGING ABDOMEN

In many men the first sign of middle age is a sagging abdomen. The abdominal muscles lose their tone and become infiltrated with fatty tissue. This causes a pulling downward of the ribs and a limitation of the breathing apparatus. In consequence the diaphragm loses much of its excursionary powers, and the organs attached to it simply drag downwards. The result is that the pressure is increased in the pelvis, and if there is any tendency to sluggishness of the bowels it will be generally made much worse.

The heavy, overloaded abdomen — and this condition may exist in otherwise quite slim men — places the bladder in a position where any small increase in the size of the gland may impede its emptying. As a matter of fact this downward pressure on the bladder tends to occlude its neck and plays as much a part in the retention of the urine as the enlargement of the prostate gland itself. If the sufferer wears a belt support he may easily add to the pelvic pressure, because anything that immobilizes the abdomen causes the weight of the organs to settle in the lower parts.

These are undoubtedly the main causative factors at work in prostate gland complaints, and if one wishes to avoid the risks of surgery later in life they must all be got into proper perspective. It is a sorry mistake to think that any such trouble arises without due cause, and in spite of the present day disregard for causative factors it is still a good philosophy to hold that cause-removal gives the most rational and certain results. It may not be the easy way; it may mean facing up to the effects of bad habits and curtailing some of the accepted pleasures that go with an indifference to health and the general welfare of the body. But the alternative is desperate remedies such as surgery, with the accompanying economic strains, which, we should still remember, may be on the state, but in fact come out of the collective pocket.

The reader may be surprised that sexual aberrations have not been named as causative factors; it remains to be said that all excesses tend to strain, and by their effect upon the whole system tend to undermine the general resistance to disease and in that sense affect the prostate gland. Apart from that, simple enlargement of the gland bears no relation to the normal sexual function.

3.

Symptoms

The symptoms of prostate trouble are usually clearly defined, and in most cases may be said to be discomfort in passing urine and a tendency to stoppage. But of course that is at a stage when very big changes have taken place in the gland, and so far as this treatise is concerned it is imperative to be warned long before such a condition arises. This is particularly one of those cases where we agree with the saying 'to be forewarned is to be forearmed'.

The diagnosis of the trouble presents very little difficulty to the practitioner. By the insertion of the finger into the rectum the enlarged prostate can be clearly felt, so that the patient's own story can be confirmed in a more certain way than with many other troubles.

But it is very late in the day when these symptoms and signs manifest themselves, and we want to help the potential sufferer to know what is going on long before such a stage is reached. These are the symptoms we wish to discuss at this point, and they are so apparently unrelated to the prostate gland that it is wise to warn the reader of their importance.

FREQUENT URINATION

One of the earliest of them, and one that is often neglected, is frequent urination. Many men put up with this sort of thing when they reach middle age because they are under the impression that it is normal to such an age. This is not a fact, and as a rule it is one of the earliest signs that there is congestion in the tissues of the gland. Some get the impression that it is because they are drinking too much fluid, and make the common error of cutting down their fluids.

Later the frequency may make the sufferer get up during the night, and even this may not prompt him to do much about it. As a matter of interest the idea is so firmly ingrained in so many men's minds that nothing less than surgery will help that they just play a futile waiting game. They tend to let things slip until the condition is well past any kind of self-treatment. They have missed nature's warning, which, had it been taken in time, might easily have saved the situation. It should be said quite emphatically that the onset of this symptom calls for active treatment because the disturbance of the night's rest in this way is in itself detrimental and will eventually undermine the resistance of the body.

Vague pains around the groins, the upper parts of the legs and lower back may be symptoms of prostatic trouble that are often mistaken for other complaints. Pain and disturbance of one part of the body are often referred to another part, and this is particularly true of prostatic troubles. Of course it may be wrong to blame the prostate gland for all the pains felt by men of middle age and older, but nothing is lost by being suspicious about it before matters have got out of hand.

Some patients complain of burning sensations in the feet and calves, together with a feeling of fullness of the veins of the legs. Tiredness and heaviness in the legs is another manifestation that should be regarded as a possible sign of trouble. When the gland is really enlarged the patient may be conscious of the enlargement and complain of a heavy feeling in the rectum which embarrasses him when he sits down.

Constipation is often a condition in its own right, but it is so frequently associated with prostate complaints that its presence should call for careful investigation. The passing of a copious mucous discharge in the urine when at stool may be a good indication that the prostate is enlarged and that the hardened faeces are pressing upon it during defecation.

SPINAL PAIN

Pains in the back and the spinal region are often experienced by those who are developing trouble with the prostate. These pains may be very clearly defined or be extremely vague. It is not unusual to find the patient complaining of a heavy feeling at the top of the spine, or, one might say, more specifically at the base of the brain. This may cause and be associated with a feeling of depression that may amount to melancholia. We should remember that it is generally accepted now that men do go through a kind of "change of life," so that ordinary symptoms may be a little exaggerated and lead to emotional upsets and broodings which the patient may find very difficult to explain to himself. In these cases it may sometimes be difficult to determine exactly whether the enlarged and irritating gland is the whole cause of the trouble or whether a difficult time of life tends to magnify the symptoms. In any case general health-building measures are of prime importance and should be instituted.

At such a time an organ such as the prostate, which is so closely associated with the emotional life and supplied with nerves that may carry reflexes to many parts of the body, will, as soon as it becomes involved in disease, disturb other parts of the nervous system. That is why a careful examination of the spine, as made by osteopaths and others, will in many cases reveal tender spots and sensitive muscles. It is not unusual to find a very painful area that seems to run right around the body parallel with the upper part of the lumbar region. When these sensitive areas first appear the patient is likely to blame the kidneys or the bowels rather than the prostate. That is why a great deal of mistaken and ineffective treatment may be undertaken at such a time.

WRONG TREATMENT
Haemorrhoids and prostate troubles are so closely associated and so likely to show similar symptoms that the wrong treatment may easily be instituted.

This is particularly true of those who think in terms of specific treatment and use medicines or remedies that are said to be 'good for' or curative of certain conditions. People who act in this way should be reminded that symptoms are very elusive and sometimes difficult to interpret correctly even to those who spend a lifetime studying them. It is clear that when specific remedies are employed the diagnosis should be accurate beyond a shadow of a doubt, otherwise the remedy will do more harm than good, or, to say the least, fail to achieve the looked-for results.

Those who believe in the healing power of the body should view the signs and symptoms which are manifested by the body in disease in a very different way from those who make use of medicines. In the latter case the idea is that the medicine will be directed against the symptom. For example, when the temperature rises an antipyretic drug will be used to lower it. Such practices leave out of account the fact that there is some causative factor behind all symptoms, and that its removal is the proper answer to the problem.

The time to make practical use of the symptoms that may be manifested is in the early stages, when structural and organic changes have not taken place. We believe that in all cases ample warning is given if we have learned to read the danger signals. This is particularly true of prostatic troubles. A patient who lets time slip by in the early stages will do so at his peril, and to be on the watch for the symptoms we have described will save disappointment later on.

4.

Water Treatment

If the reader has carefully read the foregoing chapters he will be convinced that playing a waiting game is not the right thing to do in the face of oncoming prostate complaints. One or more of the symptoms that we have described should be enough to make him realize that something should be done of a constructive nature, and taking medicine does not come within that category. Constructive measures must not merely be directed towards the alleviation of unpleasant symptoms; they must affect and improve the whole system. Although we may in the course of treatment direct measures towards a certain organ, we should never lose sight of the fact that improvement will only be real if the whole system benefits.

The reader will also be aware from the foregoing discussion that the sufferer from prostate disorders, if his treatment and physical reconstruction are to be effective, must reorganize many of his daily habits. It is a cardinal point in all Nature Cure treatment that habits must be changed. This is a sound approach, because so many of our afflictions are the result of bad habits into which we have fallen without giving much thought to their formation. Habits of eating, worrying or using our bodies are simply formed by circumstances, and by the time we are old enough to think about them, or to realize that they are important factors in the making of our infirmities, they have become so ingrained that breaking and remaking them is a well-nigh impossible task. This, of course, is where Nature Cure thinking and the ordinary practice of medicine part company: the individual must play a conscious and fully co-operative part in the plan of treatment. The idea of personal responsibility must be kept uppermost in the patient's mind.

REORGANIZING DIET

This is particularly true when we are thinking of reorganizing the patient's diet – a factor of the greatest importance in the treatment of any kind of illness. In order to do this properly the patient must be prepared to practise a good deal of self-discipline. If he is fond of a particular kind of food, or has got into the habit of eating too much of it, giving up the habit may need a lot of will-power. But if the habit is doing harm there is no other way. The same applies to the usage of the body. Habits are formed in early life which tend to strain various parts of the body, and unless something is done to rectify them their effects will disturb the normal function of various organs. These habits have to be broken and new ones acquired, and here again the individual will need to take himself in hand and go through a period of re-education.

The sufferer from prostate complaints should not regard these difficulties as just hardships but rather as blessings in disguise. These troubles rarely appear before middle age, and by that time many men have got themselves into a rut and become the slaves of their habits. If they are to face the years ahead with zest and pleasurable anticipation they need new horizons and new incentives, and trying to form new habits is perhaps the best way of stimulating the brain and the nerve pathways and filling the advancing age period with new adventures.

WATER MOST EFFECTIVE AGENT

The most effective agent in the treatment of all forms of prostate troubles is water. No matter at what stage the trouble may be, it offers to the sufferer a means of helpful relief and a safe stand-by for all emergencies. No case should go on to surgery until this simple and effective measure has been tried. There is no doubt that if it be employed resolutely in the early stages there is every chance of avoiding operative methods.

If the reader has read the chapter on the cause of the trouble and the symptoms that show themselves he should now be in a position to act without wasting precious time, and there is no doubt that the earlier he starts the better. Unlike drug treatment, the water treatment will do no harm, and even if it is used by a person who is not suffering from the complaint no damage will be done to the system. In fact it might well be undertaken by any man in middle life as a preventive measure; a week or so spent in clearing up the toxins of the system would be most useful.

The first thing we advocate in these complaints is the water diet. By this we mean that the patient should forego all solid foods and subsist for a period on water only. The ordinary individual, if he is doing this for himself, and providing he is not undertaking too strenuous an occupation, may carry this diet on for three days. The amount of water will vary with each individual, but it should be as copious as possible. There is no danger in taking a lot of water to drink providing that the stomach is empty, and this rule should be rigidly observed. Some may not be able to do this for more than one day, but it will be more effective if a full three days can be undertaken.

The water may be taken cold or hot, and it may be taken every hour or so when awake. It will greatly increase the flow through the bladder, and this is of the utmost importance. One of the greatest mistakes made by those who suffer from ailments of the uninary tract is that they tend to restrict their intake of water. It is true that if one is on an ordinary diet, taking too abundant a supply of water may lead to distension of the stomach and the bowels; but when the water is taken on an empty stomach, there is no limit to be placed on the amount that can be comfortably imbibed. But remember that the taking of solid food, no matter how small the amount, will alter the whole physiological pattern and interfere with the water diet.

As we have said, three days on the water diet is the best plan when it is undertaken as a self-treatment, but it may have to be lessened if the patient finds that too strenuous. Most patients should be able to do one day on it, but for those who feel that this is too difficult we suggest, as a minimum, the missing of a meal and taking in its place about a pint of water only, hot or cold.

As a general rule nothing should be added to the water, but we find that some patients are better able to take it if they add just enough fresh, not bottled, lemon juice, to give the water a slightly acid flavour. No sweetening, of course.

The effect of the water will be to increase the flow of urine and to empty the stomach completely. In some cases where there is a lot of stomach catarrh, the breaking down of the mucous may cause an attack of vomiting. This need not cause concern; indeed, it should be welcomed and understood as a cleansing reaction.

INTERNAL WATER TREATMENT

The enema is generally advocated in Nature Cure treatment where it is thought necessary to cleanse and stimulate the colon. In the case under discussion it should be used, both for those purposes and for direct treatment to the prostate gland. As we have already pointed out, the prostate is situated adjacent to the rectum, and when it is enlarged it may be felt to be occupying, as it were, a space of it. The congestion in it, and in the surrounding tissues, is directly affected by the faeces and their passage through the lower bowel. We may utilize this know-ledge by using the enema, therefore, not only to cleanse the parts where there have been long periods of constipation, but also to reduce the actual con-gestion within the prostate gland.

During the first three days of the water diet the enema should be used once a day to clear the lower bowel of accumulations. For this purpose we advocate a small enema of from one pint to a quart of warm water. It should be gently injected into the lower bowel and retained long enough to get a full evacuation. If only a small quantity of the water can be held, it may be repeated once or even twice. Nothing should be added to the water. The use of soap, salts, etc., is quite unnecessary.

Many people are reluctant to make use of the enema, feeling that its use is difficult and perhaps dangerous. This is a great mistake, and as it gives so great a relief and gives it quickly it is a pity not to make use of it. It is much more harmful to take purgatives and in many cases upset the whole of the alimentary tract. After a little practice with the enema the whole procedure becomes very simple, and it is much easier to carry out the operation than to describe it.

REDUCING CONGESTION

After the bowel has been thoroughly cleansed in this way we may think of using the internal water treatment as a direct means of reducing the congestion in the prostate gland. In this way hot (about 100°) and cold (as drawn from tap) applications may be made to the gland and the surrounding parts and have all the beneficial effects that they have when applied to the outside of the body. As is well known, hot and cold applications directly influence the blood and the lymph circulation. When we apply a hot application to the skin, for instance, we open the pores and relax all the underlying tissues. When we use the cold one we close the pores, cause the tissues to contract and force along the circulation. In this way we are able to influence the circulation, to stimulate the carrying away of the waste products of cell activity, and thus help to restore normal structure and function.

The irrigation of the lower bowel should be kept up until all the more immediate symptoms of the trouble have disappeared. If just plain water is employed no harm can accrue from this procedure, and where there has been long-continued constipation the thorough cleansing and stimulating action upon the walls of the rectum will prove an invaluable aid. The same treatment will be very helpful in overcoming haemorrhoids, and, as we have already explained, there is a very close connection between the two complaints.

After the alternate hot and cold applications have been used over the acute period the patient may then make use of the cold-water treatment, which is very effective in keeping the tissues of the rectum toned up and the prostate gland in a healthy, active condition. Dr Kellogg, the great authority on hydrotherapeutic measures, was an advocate of this simple plan, and other physicians, like Dr Alsaker, have used and praised the method.

COLD WATER ENEMA

The method is to inject into the lower bowel about a pint of cold water every evening before retiring. The water must be really cold, not lukewarm. It is injected as slowly as possible, and the ordinary enema is used for the purpose, and it should be retained for a period up to about thirty minutes. It may be done every night for a week, then every other night for another week and then every week-end for a month or two. Whenever there is a recurrence it may be safely resorted to.

Some people may find it rather difficult to retain it for so long, and they should go on until the retention becomes easier; or they may lessen the amount of water. When the prostate is large and flabby, with its muscular fibres very relaxed, this simple method will be found to be of the greatest value. Some have used it to the exclusion of all other methods and found it most effective, but we believe that it should be used as we have indicated: as a follow-up measure of the water diet and the cleansing effect of the enema and the hot and cold irrigation.

Apart from its beneficial effect upon the prostate gland it is of the greatest value in helping to clear up haemorrhoids and improving the general tone of the rectal tissues. As people grow old the muscles of these parts are apt to become flabby and sluggish and may be a predisposing factor in obstinate constipation. As a result, too, of taking laxatives these same tissues become congested and inactive, and thus the very remedies that are used for the cure of constipation actually produce it, and in a very difficult form. The injection of cold water is a splendid way of restoring the tone of the lower bowel, and, provided that nothing is added to the water, there is not the slightest danger in doing so.

HARMFUL MEDICINES

We mention the safety of the method because so many people, including doctors, are inclined to take the view that anything done in this way may be 'unnatural' and harmful. These same people, without the slightest hesitation, will make use of substances as medicines that are harmful to the whole length of the alimentary tract. Think for a moment of all the various drugs that are used for the treatment of headaches, colds and constipation — all taken recklessly into the much-abused stomach. We often hear of small children being killed by accidentally taking one or other of these so-called remedies, and when the result may be fatal we are told that the child took an overdose. It may be true that the young body is more susceptible to the effects of such drugs; but make no mistake about it, the adult body does not go scot-free even if the dose is supposed to be the proper one.

If we all lived natural lives, took only natural food, and used our bodies in healthy exercise, there is little doubt that we should be in less need of the treatment advocated here; but given the other conditions, sedentary occupations, sophisticated foods and the stress and strain of modern living, it is more than likely that prostate troubles and allied complaints will remain constant problems.

EXTERNAL WATER TREATMENT

Together with the water diet and the enema, the prostate may be influenced and benefited by various baths. The same principles apply, so far as the circulation of the body is concerned, as when we use the water internally. Heat relaxes the muscles: cold tones them up. Used alternately, they help in a natural way to stimulate the body and tissues to new activity and thereby get rid of the offending toxins.

We can make effective use of this knowledge in the treatment of prostate troubles.

For all pelvic troubles the alternate hot and cold sitting bath is of inestimable value, and it should be adopted by all men who suffer from prostate troubles. It is valuable because it not only gives relief to painful and distressing symptoms, but also helps to reduce congestion and to restore normal structure. It is especially helpful in relieving what is known as lymph and connective tissue stasis — a kind of constipation of the tissues — and in that way is unique as a therapeutic agent.

In a household where there is hot and cold running water — and this should be the first requisite of a real National Health Service — there will be no difficulty about applying these important measures. If there are no such arrangements for carrying out these measures then a large bowl or, better still, two large bowls may be used. Years ago, when people were more interested in hydropathic treatment, a proper portable bath was made for the purpose, and it may sometimes be possible to purchase one at a secondhand store. In some ways these specially designed baths are more useful for the purpose than the ordinary bathtub. They are made with a sloping back and a sitting arrangement so that the feet rest comfortably on the floor. They serve the admirable purpose of localizing the varying temperatures where they are required; around the pelvic area. And they are a great economy so far as the amount of water is concerned.

Whatever the arrangement may be, the idea is to sit so that the buttocks and the pelvic area generally are well covered with water. The best plan is to use hot water first and to stay in it for ten or fifteen minutes until the parts are well heated. Then have the bath or vessel emptied and filled with cold water. The cold sitting bath should not be prolonged for more than a minute or so. We stress the fact again that the heat is given to relax the tissues and the quick cold immersion tones them up.

These hot and cold sitting baths are of the greatest value when the prostate is obstructive enough to interfere with the passage of the urine, and any emergency of that kind should be met in this way. Of course these are usually neglected cases, and if the methods we are advocating here are instituted soon enough this is most unlikely to happen.

HOT AND COLD TOWELS

For those who are unable to use the alternate sitting baths, or perhaps for some reason are obliged to remain immobile, alternate hot and cold applications are advisable. Towels or suitable material are wrung out in hot water and applied for about twenty minutes or so, and then one is wrung out in cold and quickly applied. These applications may be used over the lower groin, over the lower back, between the legs and well over the anus and any other part that is adjacent to the prostate region.

These simple water treatments are worth trying in every case. It should be remembered that in years gone by, before the surgical removal of the gland was resorted to, patient treatment and nursing along these lines produced good results. The operation has come into vogue because of our present tendency to want to do everything in a hurry. No one wants to give nature a chance, but it is invariably safer to do so.

5.

Dietetic Treatment

The sufferer, having adopted the more active form of treatment that is required of her – *i.e.*, the water treatment – will now have to consider another very important subject: the reorganization of his diet and his dietetic habits. The necessity for this is very real, for it is safe to assume that 99 men out of 100 who suffer from prostate trouble will have followed the conventional methods of eating and drinking. Such feeding habits are, of course, developed in quite early childhood, and they are carried on through life without very much further thought. The result is that by the time middle age is reached such habits have crystallized into fairly rigid forms, often without any relation to the real needs of the individual.

Let us therefore consider the problem from a strictly practical point of view, so that each individual will be able to rearrange his diet so that his foods will help him to overcome the prostatic enlargement. We shall assume that the water diet has been adopted and that now he is ready to start on more solid food and to organize his diet so that the trouble may be minimized and kept at bay.

VITAMIN C DEFIENCY

If the patient has plenty of strength of will and is willing to carrying out a fairly rigorous plan of treatment we would advise him to follow the water diet with a couple of days on fruit only. This means that instead of the ordinary food the three daily meals will consist of any kind of fruit. It is a good plan to include all the fruits in season, thus ensuring that an adequate supply of vitamins are supplied to the body. There are some authorities who maintain that prostate complaints are due in part to a deficiency of vitamin C, and if this is so an adequate supply of fresh fruits will take care of it. Apart from fruits in season, apples, pears, grapefruit, grapes and fruits of a similar kind may be used to great advantage.

The exclusive fruit diet is of great value in clearing the body of the various toxins and ridding it of superfluous flesh – a common accompaniment of middle age. It means that the diet is low in starch and protein foods and abounds in the eliminative agents, and the result will be a loss of body weight, especially in relation to the superfluous tissues of the system. In middle life these waste products should be eliminated, and there is no other way of doing it without harm to the body. The use of drugs for this purpose is deprecated, and exercise will make very little impression. Those who believe that they can work off such superfluous tissues are suffering from a delusion, because it would take such strenuous efforts as are beyond the capacity of the ordinary man. A restricted diet is the only safe answer.

COOKED VEGETABLES

The exclusive fruit diet should be followed for three further days by a diet consisting of two meals of fruit and one of cooked vegetables. A good plan is to take this vegetable meal in the evening. It should be made up of all kinds of cooked vegetables, including potatoes. If these vegetables are cooked in a pressure cooker, so much the better. Or, if it is preferred, the vegetables may be made into a thick stew, which serves the same purpose. And for those who prefer to eat raw salad vegetables the meal may be made up of these in place of the cooked ones.

The general diet that should now be adopted will supply all the elements to the body and at the same time ensure easy digestion and elimination. It follows quite naturally after the fruit and vegetable diets, because these foods will still form the major part. We advocate, therefore, that the breakfast should consist, not of the conventional foods such as porridge, bacon and other cooked foods, but chiefly of fruit, which should be taken at the beginning of the meal. This should be followed by either a couple of slices of well-toasted wholemeal bread and butter or a whole product cereal of some kind. The cereal should be taken with milk and perhaps a little honey but no white sugar. Those who are satisfied with it may take only fruit and a glass of milk – quite sufficient for the physical man, though sometimes not satisfying enough for the one who has not weaned himself from his old eating habits.

The midday meal should consist of some kind of protein food, and the reader will remember that meat, fish, eggs, cheese and nuts are the principal ones. To this should be added two very nicely cooked vegetables, and these should not always include potatoes. There is an infinite variety of vegetables to choose from, and the general mistake is to ring the changes on one or two of them. It is wise when adding a dessert to this meal not to make the mistake of using heavy starchy foods, like milk pudding, suet pudding, etc. The best dessert for this meal is undoubtedly something made from fruit, either fresh or dried. This combination throws much less work on the digestion and makes a better-balanced meal.

A DAILY SALAD

The third meal of the day should be a salad meal. For the middle-aged man the eating of a daily salad is very important, and it is common experience to find that men are offenders in this respect. They appear to think that these foods are not for manly persons and eschew them. They must learn to discard this habit. Green raw foods are indispensible to all healthy people at all times; it is imperative that they should be taken when the body is labouring under difficulties such as are experienced when the prostate gland is enlarged. These vital foods contain all the essential vitamins and mineral salts in their properly balanced state. The use of salads in the daily diet will help to maintain the normal alkalinity of the blood stream and ensure the system against auto-intoxication, a condition in which the body is poisoned by its own toxins which have been too long retained within the tissues.

With the salad meal it is important to include many of the different kinds of raw vegetables that can be used in this way. The usual mistake is to limit it to one or two, say lettuce and tomatoes. Whilst both these vegetables, if grown in their natural way, are very valuable, there is a great tendency at the present time to force such vegetables, and it is questionable whether they then contain their full quota of food elements, especially the vitamins and mineral salts. The salad, therefore, should contain all kinds of raw vegetables, and we advocate the use of the various herbs in this way. One of the problems of using the term 'herbs' is that many people think of them only as medicines. This is a great pity, because they can and should be used as important foods. Thus the salad may be enlarged and greatly increased in value by adding such herbs as sage, balm, cabbage (especially valuable in the winter), corn salad, chives, chicory, dandelion, endive, fennel, the various cresses, nasturtium leaves and flowers, rosemary flowers (not leaves) and so on. Many of these plants are grown in the garden but are rarely used as they should be. An enterprising housewife, with a little forethought, can add all kinds of variety to the salad; and whilst improving its flavour add also to its food value. The various herbs can also be added to soups to enrich them and to heighten their flavour.

As a general rule salads are best enjoyed with foods that need thorough mastication, and stale or well-toasted wholewheat bread answers the purpose. This, together with cheese, makes a perfect meal. Whilst they do not require quite so much mastication, we may say that well-baked potatoes are also a perfect addition. The rule to observe is that salad needs and enforces mastication, and, therefore, taking starchy foods at the same time is very wise because they too must be well chewed in order to facilitate digestion.

The three-meal plan which we have described will work well with cases of enlarged prostate and will ensure an adequate and well-balanced diet. It does not limit the foods in any way. There are, however, certain foods that should be definitely avoided. Those who are middle-aged or over need to cut down starchy foods, and of these white flour is one of the worst. Apart from the fact that bleaching and other forms of preparation make it into a very doubtful form of food, it enters into so many made-up dishes and tends therefore to overload the diet with starch. The middle-aged man will, with real advantage to himself, cut down the use of this flour to the bare minimum.

The same applies to white sugar, which is so often used in conjunction with white flour. Together they are a serious menace. Such dishes should be studiously avoided, especially by those who have passed their youth. Condiments also should be avoided, and whenever there is vinegar added they should not be put in the category of food. Salt may be taken in moderation, but, as will have been observed, the special diets eliminate this substance for a while, which is a good plan.

RULES FOR EATING

So much for the food itself. Now what about the rules governing the use of it? They are generally well known but not often observed, and will bear repeating time and time again.

First: Never eat unless there is a keen relish for food.

Second: Never eat when overtired.

Third: Never eat if uncomfortable in mind or body.

Fourth: Never eat when any organ of the body is functionally disturbed.

Fifth: Never eat when hurried or excited.

Sixth: Never eat immediately before great emotional nervous or physical strain.

Seventh: Never eat immediately before going to sleep.

Those are the negative rules. Let us turn to the more constructive ones:

Chew your food thoroughly and slowly. Try to taste the various flavours of foods. Many people swallow food without knowing one taste from another. Tasteless food means badly prepared food, and condiments are not the proper answer. The use of condiments is condemned if for no other reason than that they allow badly prepared and insipid food to be swallowed. A good cook knows when not to cook and imparts into the preparation of food as much art and creative expression as knowledge and hard work.

A final word on beverages. Water is the great solvent, the real thirst-quencher, and should be taken apart from food. When anything is added to water it becomes a food, and not a drink. Tea, sugar, milk,

cocoa, malted milk, coffee, and the hundred and one
things that we add to it change its nature and call into
action the digestive juices. For example, a cup of
cocoa should be regarded as a part of a meal, and
should not be sandwiched in between as a drink.
Water is the drink that should be taken between
meals, and, generally speaking, not at meal times.
These rules are of the greatest significance to the
sufferer from prostate troubles, who should heed
them carefully.

5.

Exercise and Postural Training

The foregoing chapters will have shown the reader
that his problems will be solved only by the most
strict attention to daily habits, by the use of suitable
measures for the relief of the congestion and by a
rigid adherence to sensible methods of eating. We
now turn to a very important aspect of the whole
problem, which every individual must be prepared to
study and understand if he would make his return to
full health and normal function successful.

THE MECHANICAL ASPECT

We refer to the subject from what might be termed
the mechanical aspect. A little thought will convince
anyone that the human body is liable to mechanical
strains, especially in relation to its upright position.
Balancing ourselves, as we do, on two legs, leaves us
under much greater gravitational strain than, for
example, the quadruped. In early life it takes quite a
long period of self-training and time before we are
able to adapt ourselves to this position, and, as we

grow old, and our vitality and resistance decrease, we maintain it only with effort, and the strain finally is too much for us. The struggle to maintain the upright line of health becomes too hard when age has taken its toll.

In middle life the first signs of these strains make themselves manifest. The way in which so many people live, the bad positions assumed in various occupations, the effects of accidents, and many other factors reduce the capacity of the body to struggle against the forces of gravity, and the bent shoulders, the strained spine, the bad position of the head and neck, which are so often seen in middle age, are the first signs that the body is giving under strain. The ribs begin to fall forward and no longer act as springs for the abdominal muscles. These muscles lose their tone and sag forward, and all the organs of the abdomen gradually tend to fall downwards and upon the pelvic area. Many people, thinking that such a condition is an inevitable accompaniment of middle life, have named it the middle-age spread.

FUNCTIONAL CHANGES

Such a change in the structure of the body is bound to bring with it functional changes, which, if they continue over a prolonged period, will produce structural changes also. Here we have one of the prime causes of prostate complaints, and one that is rarely thought about by those who suffer from them, or, for that matter, by those who treat them. Until the advent of osteopathy, which stresses as its fundamental principle the importance of the mechanical factors in the body, no branch of medicine seemed to pay any attention to such an idea.

Yet all the factors we have described are in constant and harmful operation. In middle life the body begins to lose its ability to maintain the erect position, and normal balance becomes a struggle against considerable odds. The contents of the abdomen come under the heaviest strain, and finally adjust themselves at a great disadvantage, strained and low down on the pelvic region. This means that the bladder and the prostate no longer have the freedom of movement that is consistent with an erect and agile body. The result is that there is now every possible chance that the immobility of the pelvic organs will produce congestion in all the structures and tissues.

The position of the bladder changes in its relationship to other parts, and it is easy to realize that even its emptying will be at a great disadvantage. The pressure of the organs from above will definitely tend to 'kink' the organ and to make its complete emptying much more difficult, and the prostate gland is sometimes blamed for an obstruction that may be caused in this way. With the changed and lowered position of the organs above it the bladder tends to be pressed downwards so that the lower part of it empties with difficulty when the body is in the erect position. The retention of urine in this way leads to many of the irritating symptoms that are associated with prostatic enlargement. This is the reason for adoption of the special position of the body when emptying the bladder, which we shall advocate later for sufferers from prostate troubles.

WARNING SIGNALS

From these observations it will be noted that the proper posture of the body is of the greatest importance, especially in middle life, and whilst we say that in prostatic enlargement no treatment is thoroughly complete that does not take this important point into consideration, it is such a vital subject in middle age that every person should pay some attention to it. If you want to maintain your normal activity late into life, make posture-training a 'must' as soon as age begins to make itself felt. For men there are three signs that should waken his interest in his failing powers: greying hair, the drooping spine and an awareness of the difficulty in passing urine. These are, of course, the warning signals of middle age.

Posture training, as such, is in many ways a new idea in the treatment of any kind of bodily disorder, and should not be confused with the old notion of physical culture. In those so-called systems of physical training the chief idea was to train the muscles, and the various groups of these were identified and developed and sometimes over-developed. Very little attention was paid to the joints or to the balance of the body as a whole, so that if the individual could pose in some curious way that would exaggerate his muscles, everybody seemed to be satisfied. It was this kind of thing that scared away many people who thought that the whole set-up was allied to the making of strong men and music-hall stunts.

Medical men who observed these individuals came to the conclusion that such training did not help very much in building up the bodily health and resistance, and that is why, no doubt, the medical men, as a group, tend to disparage physical culture as a method of treating ailments and preventing disease. On the other hand the osteopath concentrated his whole attention on the spinal column, and soon realized that strongly muscled individuals were almost as liable to lesions of that part of the body as others, and that exercise along the ordinary lines did not necessarily produce a well-balanced and well-integrated spine.

CENTRE OF MOTIVATING POWER

The finding of lesions in the spinal column and the realization that these lesions could produce functional disturbance elsewhere made the osteopath aware of the importance of the mechanics of the body. He realized, too, that whilst the muscles played a big part in maintaining the equilibrium of the system there was no doubt that the skeletal parts, and particularly the joints, deserved the most careful consideration. These findings led naturally to the fact that as the spine was the centre of the motivating power of the body, and thus very closely associated with the great nervous system, any disturbance that affected it was bound to upset the balancing apparatus and lead to stress and strain.

It followed from this that apart from the ordinary stresses of daily life, the mental and the emotional ones, there existed the possibility of very great stress and strain through the effect of the mechanical forces upon the body, and so posture took on a new meaning altogether. It was not merely the habit of standing upright with the feet out-turned and chest drawn up, as illustrated in the old text-books on training and gymnastics; it was a matter of proper balance of the body, plus the correlation of all the various organs and systems and the integration of the nervous system. In brief, next to the importance of air, light and food, man's proper relationship with the mechanical forces surrounding him was of real survival value.

When we are able to translate these principles into practical therapeutics many individuals will be able to enjoy the benefits of well-being on a scale hitherto not known, because we shall then turn from the fallacies of medication to the whole body-and-mind technique; and we shall see that the removal of organs such as the prostate gland, tonsils and so on is merely a confession of our failure to appreciate that the parts of the body are as important as the whole, and exist in separate divisions not in fact but merely as a concept in our minds. That we are able to live without them after such organs have been removed proves the resourcefulness of nature, not our ability to outwit and conquer her.

THREE CHIEF POINTS

All forms of posture training should begin with three chief points in mind: balancing the head on the top of the spine, the spine as a whole and the feet. It may be wise to say a few things about these parts of the body and to emphasize their significance, especially in relation to pelvic troubles, the chief of which in middle-aged men is the prostate enlargement. If this relationship is a new idea to the reader he should not make the mistake of under-estimating it.

Balancing the head on the top of the spine is a piece of engineering that we take very much for granted, and yet it is a masterpiece of ingenuity. A properly balanced head is the hall-mark of physical efficiency, and, conversely, one that is not is an infallible sign of lowered resistance and ill-health. The reason for this is largely mechanical. When the head is easily balanced there is no strain on any part of the body, but when it is not, many muscles and other structures are brought under strain. In and about the joint that holds the head at the top of the spine there are some twenty muscles, and all these are constantly used in every movement of the head and body. This alone should impress us with the extent of the strain when the head is working under unfavourable conditions.

But the movement of the head is not only a muscular action: the position of the head in space and its relation to every changed position of the body

s a reflex action, and if strain of the head-spine
relationship occurs, some degree of the efficiency of
this reflex action will be lost, and the whole body will
suffer in consequence. In the normal balance of the
body the head must always be adjusted over the
centre point, and every movement of the body — like
walking up and down stairs, for example — is so much
the easier for this quick and unconscious adjustment.
When it has slowed down through any reason our
movements will be awkward and cumbersome.

FUNCTIONS UNDER STRAIN

In brief, all the spinal curves lose their dynamic
quality and tend at certain points to become fixed.
As the curves are exaggerated, as they will be under
strain, the whole supporting structure of the body is
weakened. The body weight is carried at a great
disadvantage, and all the functions of the system are
performed under a certain amount of strain. The
muscles of the body, in particular, having lost their
proper position by virtue of the change in the body
structure, lose their tone, and many organs of the
body, especially those in the abdominal region, sag
and become favourably placed for disorders of all
kinds.

The final result of this physical inefficiency is seen
in the feet. The feet are weight-bearing, and if there is
an undue strain from above they break down under
it. They tend to splay out, and the weight of the
body falls on to the inside of the feet, placing too
much strain at this point. Another result of this
condition is that the hips tend to turn outwards, thus
letting the belly drop forward and downwards — the
typical picture of middle and older age.

These are the tendencies that the prospective
sufferer has to face, and the sooner he recognizes
them the better for his future prospects. He has got

to make up his mind to reverse them — that is to say, to restore, by careful usage of his body, its balance and its mechanical efficiency.

CORRECTING BAD POSTURE

In correcting the bad habits of posture he has acquired the patient should start by analysing his own body in the light of the foregoing remarks. Then, having noted the weak points and the offending structures, he must proceed to rectify them. A helpful plan is to stand in front of a mirror and observe with a critical eye the way in which the body is carried and balanced. Then lie on the floor on the back with the legs fully extended. In this position many of the weak points of a bad posture will be brought into relief. For example, if, in the standing position, the head is carried too far forward, the tendency will be for the top rather than the back of the head to rest on the floor. Also, if the spinal curves are exaggerated and fixed, lying flat on the back may give quite a lot of pain in the muscle, especially if the position is retained for ten minutes or so.

Lying flat on the floor at the end of the day is one of the best exercises for posture correction. It gradually straightens out the back, pushes the neck into its normal position and takes the weight off the feet so that they may relax. But it must be on a hard surface: lying on a bed or a soft divan will be of no use whatsoever.

After lying on the back with the legs extended for about ten minutes the lower part of the back may begin to ache. This may be due to the strain placed on the muscles that pass through the pelvis and which, when in the standing position, transfer the weight-bearing from the trunk to the legs. By drawing the feet up to the buttocks this strain can be lessened and the pull on the lower spine released. This is a very important point for those who have prostate troubles, because the releasing of this strain is of direct help in relieving congestion. At the same time this position takes the strain off the abdominal muscles and allows the contents of the abdomen to move more freely than when in the standing position. With all this strain relieved another important point may be noted: the diaphragm also becomes much more freely movable. This movement can be increased by deep breathing, and the diaphragm will then tend to pull the abdominal organs up towards the chest.

FLOOR AS SUPPORT

Breathing in this way releases the tension on the back, lifts the pelvic organs and restores the proper angle to the ribs. As a matter of fact we are using the floor as a kind of support, so that the bent and tired body can go through the movements that it should go through when in the proper erect position. We cannot over-estimate the importance of this simple way of correcting bad posture and relieving the congestion in the lower abdominal area of the body, and the reader should practise it with great care and persistence.

At the same time it does two very important things: it corrects the bad posture and it enables the performer to relax thoroughly. Today we hear a great deal about the need for relaxation, and there is no doubt that it is of the greatest importance; but it must be done in the right way. It is of little use trying to relax if there is great tension on the spine, if the head is held in a strained position and if the ribs and the abdominal muscles are cramped together with their normal movement impeded. If the above instructions are followed to the letter the most tense person will find that the strain will be gradually relieved and that all the muscles will fall into easy positions, so that the tenseness will no longer exist.

The mind also will be relieved, because when the muscles are tense and on the jump the mind will be too. It is a vicious circle; the mind normally releases its pent-up energy through muscular action, but when there is neither a proper direction of mental energy nor a proper action of the muscles the result is that there is great irritability in both. That is the state of affairs when a so-called nervous breakdown is imminent or actually occurs, and people who suffer in this way are told that they should relax. It is true that they should, but in ninety-nine times out of a hundred they just cannot do it. The art of relaxation can be learned only by following a plan that corrects the faulty posture, and then it follows almost automatically.

DRAINED PELVIS

The patient should now be in a fairly relaxed state with the back resting comfortably on the floor, the neck straight and the breathing easy and full. The next position is to raise the pelvic part of the body as high as possible, and to put under it a hard cushion or some object that will hold it as comfortably high as possible, thus making a straight line from the knees to the chest. In this position the pelvis is considerably higher than the upper part of the abdomen, and there is a natural tendency for the contents of the pelvis to be drained and relieved. Rhythmic breathing may be continued so as to stimulate the movements of the inner organs, and as a useful adjunct to this the patient may try consciously to relax and contract the abdominal muscles.

This position is of great value in taking the weight and strain off the bladder and the prostate gland, and should be held for about ten minutes or even longer if possible. Incidentally, this position is of great help in cases of piles and of prolapsed organs of either sex.

This position may be usefully varied by taking the cushion or support from under the buttocks and then raising the pelvis up and down slowly as an exercise. Place the hands under the lower back, and try to push the pelvis up as high as possible. Then place the support under the buttocks again after doing the exercise about six times or so. Relax for a few minutes before changing to the next position.

Now assume the first position of lying completely flat on the back with the legs extended flat on the floor. Bend the knees, and bring them up as high as possible towards the head. Place the hands on the outside of the knees, and then pull the knees as high as they will come. If this is done properly the buttocks will be lifted slightly off the floor. This is very important, because it tends to rock the pelvis.

KICKING AN IMAGINARY OBJECT

Release the hands from the knees, and shoot out both legs, as though kicking an imaginary object suspended in the air. Do not do this too vigorously at first, because it is apt to strain the abdominal muscles; but after a while a certain control will be developed over the movement, and it may be done with a good deal of speed. It is one of the most useful of all such exercises, because it tends to shake up the contents of the pelvis and the jerk of the feet transmits an upward force through that region. The good effect of this movement in activating a sluggish bowel makes its practice well worth while.

It is also one of the best ways of relieving the circulation in the legs, and it should be done to help clear the pressure from the veins in the lower parts of the body. It helps to overcome haemorrhoids, and where the piles have 'come down' it will tend to pull them back into their normal position. It should be repeated several times, according to the strength and energy of the patient. By doing it a few times and then relaxing it can be continued for a few minutes without undue strain. It is almost a specific for relieving congestion in the bladder and the prostate gland, and should not be omitted. It places a good deal of strain on the abdominal muscles, so where the patient has a large and ponderous waist line due caution should be observed at the start of the training. But if the exercise is practised assiduously it will tone up the muscles and reduce the girth very much better than almost any other form of exercise.

ELBOWS-KNEES POSITION

After going through these movements very carefully the patient should now assume the elbows-knees position, which is a kneeling posture with the front part of the body supported on the elbows. In this position the whole structure of the body has been completely changed from that of lying on the back. The head tends to fall forward, and the curves of the spine, not having any support, drop lower in the lumbar region and are more rounded in the upper part of the trunk. In the relaxed condition try to allow these curves to fall as much as possible into an easy position.

Now begin to rock the body backwards and forwards on the knees and elbows. Do this for a few minutes, as relaxed as possible; simply allow the body to fall forward on its own weight, and then with as little effort as possible take it back on to the haunches. Then gradually begin to put some effort into the movement, trying to go forward as far and as quickly as possible, and the same in the reverse position.

The effect of this movement is to shake up the abdominal contents and to take the weight off the pelvic organs. It has often been used for the relief of prolapsed organs, and it will be readily understood after doing it a few times how effective it can be. Between the movements, when getting tired, the performer may rest with the head on the hands. This knee-chest position, which is a well-known method of relieving congestion in the pelvic region, allows the body to relax in a very comfortable position, with the head and spine relieved of any undue tension.

Next the patient should adopt the hands-and-toes position, in which the weight of the body is supported on the hands and the toes. This may be the starting point for many useful movements. The first may be to affect the spine by dropping the middle of the body as near to the floor as possible. From this position also one may walk forward with the feet, keeping the hands in a fixed position, and this will tend to arch the back — again a useful movement for the spine. In this quadruped position one may then attempt to walk round on all fours and thus stimulate the organs of the lower abdomen.

Finish the exercises by sitting back on your haunches in a kind of squatting position, and then come into the erect position.

The effect of all these movements will be to limber up the spine and pull the whole body into a better condition, so that the performer should have a feeling of freshness about him. It is a very good plan to use a mirror to see how many of the old postural mistakes have been corrected by this simple training method. Of course they will all tend to reappear if the old habits are adopted, but if the exercise is done regularly and an awareness of the bad postural habits developed, the changes can be made permanent and will be of the greatest assistance in improving the health of the whole body, in addition to restoring the function of the various organs.

EXERCISE A THERAPEUTIC AGENT

The value of such exercise as a therapeutic agent is
often overlooked, because there is a general belief
that few people will practise it long enough and with
enough care to make it effective. But next to an
adequate and well-arranged diet, exercise offers one
of the best and most natural ways of stimulating
sluggish organs into activity and thus enabling the
body to restore its normal functions.

There is, in fact, no substitute for properly
directed exercise. Some people, lacking the energy
and the will to carry it out, have tried substitutes, and
one generally adopted is massage. We believe that
every experienced practitioner, and particularly
orthopaedic authorities, would agree that this should
only be substituted when the individual is unable to
carry out movements for himself. Massage stimulates
the superficial circulation and loosens up the
muscular fibres, but it cannot reach into the inner
parts like active exercise. For example, in positioning
the body as we have described and using the
expansive power of the lungs, we increase the
excursions of the diaphragm. In this way the
abdominal organs are moved thoroughly and given a
kind of internal message, the like of which no external
massage could accomplish.

SKIN LIFTING

As an adjunct to exercise we advise, not the ordinary
kind of self-massage that is sometimes suggested, but
a method of stimulating the connective tissue just
beneath the skin. The connective tissues hold many
of the waste products of the body and are related to
the blood and the lymph circulation. One way of
stimulating this great system is by lifting and squeez-
ing the skin. The skin should be firmly grasped and
lifted, to free it as much as possible. When one is in

good health the skin of the body is freely movable; in disease the skin tightens and loses its elasticity. Much can be done to liven up its circulation by lifting and pinching it, and after exercise it is most helpful. Also it is of great value when undertaking a hot bath.

7.

General Advice

The reader will not need to be reminded that prostate disorders are closely associated with the passing of the urine from the body, and it may now be a good plan to go a little more fully into this function so that its significance may be realized. The body has several depurating systems — that is to say, systems that remove from the body the waste products of its activity. The lungs, the bowels, the skin, and the kidneys are of the greatest importance in this respect, and it is easy to understand that any interference with their normal functions must be of real danger to the whole of the system.

The chief organs in this depurating system are, of course, the kidneys, and the bladder is used mostly as a storage for the urine that comes from them. The blood passes through the kidneys, and it is the function of the latter to separate from it the waste products that are no longer required in the system. How this interchange of blood, fluids and waste takes place within the kidney is still a problem that puzzles many physiologists, but for the ordinary person it is enough to know how important it is that it should be carried on normally.

If we partake of an excessive amount of liquid it will be the function of the kidneys to see that the normal amount be retained in the blood stream, and to that end the kidneys will assist the body in maintaining its balance. The kidneys are also closely associated with the skin, and share with it the excretion of water and some waste products.

From these brief notes it will be seen how important it is that nothing should interfere with the regular elimination of the urine from the body. The urinary apparatus is richly supplied with nerves, and disturbance of its function is quickly reflected in the general nervous system. It follows that when the urination function is delayed or impeded in any way there is a direct threat to the integrity of the kidneys.

When the urine is separated in the kidneys it seeps down the ureters – small membraneous tubes – until it reaches the bladder. The flow down these tubes may differ from time to time. It may be decreased when fasting and increased after meals; it may be increased also after taking large amounts of fluid. Finally it reaches the bladder through tiny sphincter valves which prevent a return flow. The bladder in time accumulates enough fluid to set in motion certain reflexes which excite its emptying. The act of urination may be performed voluntarily, that is without waiting until the nervous reflex is stimulated by the pressure in the bladder, and many who do so probably only occasionally allow the bladder to distend itself.

DIFFICULTY IN URINATING

This act is closely allied to the nervous system, so that nervousness may interfere with the act. In some cases an attack of nerves or great excitement may actually make urination difficult in an otherwise normal case, and it has been found that the sound of running water or putting the hands in water will restore the normal function. If the nerves have been paralysed then of course the control is lost, and the urine may leak when the bladder is filled to its capacity.

In the normal body it is clear that the constituents of the urine will be so balanced that the bladder may maintain it without any difficulty; but when, as in certain forms of disease, the waste products that leave the body in this way are excessive or of a toxic nature, the walls of the bladder will be adversely affected. In cystitis (inflammation of the bladder), for example, the irritation may be caused by urine that contains excessive toxic substances which set up disorders of the membranes. Then, of course, there will be over-excitement of the reflexes and constant desire to void the urine.

Similarly, if the urine, especially if its toxic constituents are high, is retained too long it will cause irritation. This is what occurs in prostatic troubles, when there is an interference with the normal emptying and a residue of the urine remains. This will mean great frequency, because the bladder will never be fully relieved and the urine will become more loaded with toxins.

In early life the flow of the urine is very vigorous, but as age creeps on this flow is considerably diminished. The use of places where there is a tendency for this flow to be restricted may play some part in diminishing the capacity of it and be a real factor in the dribbling effects of old age. And also emptying the bladder by doing it at certain times without waiting for the reflex to operate may in time reduce the efficiency of the reflex through lack of usage.

The bad effect that may follow these practices is that the bladder, especially when middle life is reached, is never properly emptied. We may make a comparison with the bowel in this respect. Many people suffer in later life from bowel disorders because they have placed bowel elimination too much under voluntary control and developed as a result a sluggish and ineffective method of defecation. As a matter of fact, individuals who suffer from the one complaint invariably suffer from the other; yet many people who are concerned about the lack of efficiency in the emptying of the bowel, and who are for ever taking drugs to stimulate the function, scarcely give a thought to the same condition in the bladder – until an emergency arises.

BLADDER EMPTYING

Fully emptying the bladder is more important – if there is any sense in making such a comparison – than fully emptying the lower bowel. The erect position of the body places the bladder in a position where is is liable to sag into the pelvis and to form a pocket where residual urine is likely to collect. The irritation that this may cause in the region of the prostate gland may be an unsuspected cause of some of the congestion that finally leads to prostate enlargement.

As a corollary to this it has been found in practice that it is a good plan for those who are at an age where the latter complaint is likely to develop to pay special attention to the act of fully emptying the bladder, and it is advised that every evening before retiring the bladder should be emptied in the quadruped or all-fours position. A suitable vessel should be used, and the act should not be hurried. If the pelvis can be elevated a little, so much the better. Careful attention to this way of urination just before sleep often results in a night's rest without the usual interruption.

It has been shown that exercise stimulates the kidneys and the production of urine, so that it is a good plan to carry out the exercises already described ust before retiring, so that the bladder may then be properly drained. We desire to emphasize the importance of emptying the bladder in this way, especially if any symptoms of prostate enlargement have shown themselves.

COMPLETE STOPPAGE

A word will be in place here about cases where, after years of unheeded warning signals, the emergency of complete stoppage occurs. Such a condition calls for prompt attention, because without it the bladder would soon distend to the point of rupture and the kidneys would cease in their important functions. Such a condition could not be tolerated for very long without disastrous results. This is the kind of condition that needs help and calls for the immediate attention of the experienced practitioner, who will use a catheter to draw away the urine.

In the meantime, and where less effective help is needed, the hot relaxing bath should be tried. The patient should be put into a full bath of hot water and remain there until the body is relaxed. Such a procedure may relieve the worst cases, but there must be no undue delay in taking the pressure from the bladder. Let it be said, however, that such emergencies do not arise without warning, and 'a stitch in time will save nine'.

Such cases, when they have run on to where they may need desperate remedies, have invariably been backed by years of habits which have undermined the capacity of the body to preserve its normal function. It is not suggested that such habits are wilful in the sense that the individual knows what he is doing to himself and damns the consequences. On the contrary, practically all such cases are due to ignorance, and we charge the medical profession with a certain amount of dereliction of duty towards many of these

individuals. They have acted as they have because
they have been completely unaware of any harm in
the many habits they have built up, and they believe
that disease is a condition that strikes them from out of
the blue. It is also unfortunately true that such
habits are exploited commercially, so that to expose
the results to critical and public analysis is very
difficult.

THE SMOKING HABIT

Let us take the smoking habit as an example of what
we mean. There is little doubt that this is harmful
especially if carried to excess. In some cases it does
much more harm than in others. For example, it is
held by some to play a big part as a causative factor
in producing cancer of the lungs, and there can be no
doubt that when an individual has a pre-disposition to
any disease, any habit that tends to undermine the
general health is a positive danger to the *particular
individual,* and his doctor, who should be conversant
with his family history and any disease diathesis that
may exist, would warn him in the plainest possible
terms.

Apart from direct harm to the system which may
occur from smoking and the intake of foreign
substances, there is the strain it throws on the system
through the development, in some cases, of the
violent coughing bouts. Although very little attention
has ever been paid to this aspect of the problem it is
by no means insignificant. In families where there is a
hereditary tendency to the development of hernia
there can be no doubt that the strain of coughing
may be a very real factor in breaking down the
resistance of the abdominal wall. A *family* doctor, if
he would live up to that important title, should warn
the members of such families of the dangers that
smoker's cough may have in such cases.

In the complaints that we are discussing in this book there is no doubt that smoking is a habit that should be abandoned or indulged in with great circumspection. The effect of constant coughing is to drive the abdominal and pelvic organs low in their cavities and directly to promote congestion – the first stage in prostate enlargement. If the individual wants confirmation of this, let him stand before a mirror and watch the effects of violent coughing on the abdominal muscles. Then there is the harmful effect of the nicotine itself. We know that it has an effect on the nervous system, and through the system on the heart, which produces smoker's heart in some individuals.

Next in importance to the nervous system stands the glandular tissue in the body. We have no authoritative knowledge of the effect of nicotine on this. In a vague way many thinkers have a notion that smoking tends to reduce fertility in the human, both female and male; and if this is so, it may well be because of its effects on the important glandular tissues connected with this function. We cannot, therefore, rule out the possibility that excessive smoking may be a very potent cause of prostate disorder and enlargement, and every thoughtful man should give this matter his earnest consideration. Dr Starr White, who has had much experience in the disease, is very emphatic. He says: 'I do not believe any case of prostatic disease can be cured while nicotine and/or alcohol is in the system.'

WORRY

The stress of modern life brings with it problems that weigh heavily on the shoulders of those who are perhaps less fortunate in the struggle we have come to believe is the common lot. Few people live without some kind of strain, and if it goes on without relief it is bound to lead to all kinds of physical and mental tensions. Out of such a condition we build the health-destroying habit of worrying. The dictionary definition of worry is given as 'to tease, to harass,' and when the habit of worrying is in the saddle that is just what we do to ourselves. Worry does no good, of course, and it enervates the nervous system and in that way builds ill-health.

Those who believe that germs are the cause of most ill-health find it difficult to explain how worry contributes to the making of disease. Those who practise medicine do not use a specific that will 'cure' worry; not even the homoeopaths, who certainly can claim the record for the number of remedies they employ. Yet there is no doubt that worry is the great wrecker of body and mind. Of course it is not a first cause in itself. Behind it we have many other factors operating — social, economic and environmental. We even have the burdens of heredity that instil worry and the fear that goes with it into the hearts of men. We have the worry of wars, of upheavals, of impending events and all contribute in some measure to the making of individual and social ill-health.

Worry is not only the concern of the individual. No one can sit aside and pretend that he is happy and serene in his own soul whilst there is so much suffering and strife in the world, and we deceive ourselves if we think that we can live our lives apart from the lives of others. In the physical world we must share in the environment that we build up for ourselves. One has only to think of the food and water supplies to realize that we are not entirely free agents. It is a moot point whether, when disease is brought upon us by social and economic disturbances and injustices, we as individuals can hope wholly to escape from them. The diseases that follow wars become endemic, and for all we know they affect, in some measure, every one of us.

MENTAL ENVIRONMENT

This is peculiarly true of mental environment. Our minds are not watertight compartments isolated from the rest of the world. They are delicate instruments that are tuned in with the whole human family and share in the waves of thought, that, like the waves of the sea, keep breaking in on our consciousness. There is a social mind as well as an individual mind, and we are all affected by the varied developments that take place around us.

In all forms of disease, in all the changes that take place in our bodies as a result of them, there is an interaction with our minds. This cycle in the body-and-mind relationship may operate either way for the development of disease. We may build disease through wrong physical habits, and we may do it through the mind. Worry, grief and mental tension enervate the nervous system and leave all the functions of the body without the vital energy to carry on. The result is a breakdown at the weakest point.

The right mental environment is therefore as important as the proper physical one, and we should all do our part in trying to build a better one, not only for ourselves, but for the rest of the peoples in the world. There are wise philosophers who have contended that the only way in which we may succeed in this respect is by thinking first of others, and that is why we need, at this time in our history perhaps more than any other, to make health, wholeness of mind and body, the common ideal. In these terms we realize that we cannot get such a condition from a bottle of medicine, or from a surgical operation, or, indeed, from the discoveries of scientists who see little farther than their own noses. We shall get it by making the world a better place to live in, so that the human body may carry out all its functions with all its organs intact, including those that surgeons now cleverly remove — the tonsils, the ovaries, the prostate. Then we shall be on the right road to a fuller and richer life.

RÉSUMÉ

As a brief reminder to the reader of what he should have in mind for the proper management of his complaint we append the following short outline. He should put the plan into operation at the first sign of the trouble, or, indeed, if he has reached an age when the prostate may be a suspected associative factor in his lack of good health.

Adopt the water diet from one to three days.

Follow this with the fruit diet from one to three days.

Continue a further one to three days on the special vegetable and fruit diet.

Then adopt a carefully planned general diet.

Use the enema to cleanse and stimulate the lower bowel.

Use hot (about 100 degrees) and cold (as drawn from the tap) water irrigations in the lower bowel.

Follow with the cold water (as drawn from the tap) injections into the lower bowel.

Use the alternate hot (as reasonably hot as can be borne) and cold (as drawn from the tap) water sitting baths.

Adopt the special positioning exercises, and then make a careful analysis of the body in relation to general usage, occupation, etc.

Overhaul all the various habits that have been unconsciously built up, and try to correct or modify them and thus reduce the strain on the nervous system and the general health.